-ack as in snack

Pam Scheunemann

Consulting Editor Monica Marx, M.A./Reading Specialist

ABDO
Publishing Company

Published by SandCastle™, an imprint of ABDO Publishing Company, 4940 Viking Drive, Edina, Minnesota 55435.

Credits
Edited by: Pam Price
Curriculum Coordinator: Nancy Tuminelly
Cover and Interior Design and Production: Mighty Media
Photo Credits: Brand X Pictures, Corbis Images, Digital Vision, Eyewire Images, Hemera, PhotoDisc, Stockbyte

Library of Congress Cataloging-in-Publication Data

Scheunemann, Pam, 1955-
    -Ack as in snack / Pam Scheunemann.
        p. cm. -- (Word families. Set VI)
    Summary: Introduces, in brief text and illustrations, the use of the letter combination "ack" in such words as "snack," "track," "lack," and "quack."
    ISBN 1-59197-261-2
    1. Readers (Primary) [1. Vocabulary. 2. Reading.] I. Title.

PE1119 .S434 2003
428.1--dc21   2002038222

SandCastle™ books are created by a professional team of educators, reading specialists, and content developers around five essential components that include phonemic awareness, phonics, vocabulary, text comprehension, and fluency. All books are written, reviewed, and leveled for guided reading, early intervention reading, and Accelerated Reader® programs and designed for use in shared, guided, and independent reading and writing activities to support a balanced approach to literacy instruction.

Let Us Know

After reading the book, SandCastle would like you to tell us your stories about reading. What is your favorite page? Was there something hard that you needed help with? Share the ups and downs of learning to read. We want to hear from you! To get posted on the ABDO Publishing Company Web site, send us e-mail at:

sandcastle@abdopub.com

SandCastle Level: Beginning

-ack Words

back

black

sack

snack

stack

track

Ray has his back to the
shore.

Spot is black and
white.

Bill wants to win the
sack race.

Rita eats an apple for a snack.

Shawn likes to stack
the blocks.

Jake runs fast on the track.

The Sack
Out Back

Eve is a girl
who wears
all black.

One day out back,
she found a sack.

13

Out of the sack
came a coat rack.

Then out of the sack
came a jack.

Eve almost
had an attack
when she
saw a track
come out
of the sack!

Now there
was a rack,
a jack,
and a railroad track!

Next came a duck,
who said quack!

Then Eve saw
blocks in a stack.

Seeing all
that stuff
come out
of the sack
made Eve
so hungry
she had
a snack.

The -ack Word Family

attack	sack
back	shack
black	slack
jack	snack
lack	stack
pack	tack
quack	track
rack	whack

Glossary

Some of the words in this list may have more than one meaning. The meaning listed here reflects the way the word is used in the book.

sack   a bag made of paper

snack   a small amount of food eaten between meals

stack   a pile of things placed one on top of the other; to put things in a pile

track   an oval path that cars, horses, or people race around; a set of rails for trains to run on

About SandCastle™

A professional team of educators, reading specialists, and content developers created the SandCastle™ series to support young readers as they develop reading skills and strategies and increase their general knowledge. The SandCastle™ series has four levels that correspond to early literacy development in young children. The levels are provided to help teachers and parents select the appropriate books for young readers.

Emerging Readers
(no flags)

Beginning Readers
(1 flag)

Transitional Readers
(2 flags)

Fluent Readers
(3 flags)

These levels are meant only as a guide. All levels are subject to change.

To see a complete list of SandCastle™ books and other nonfiction titles from ABDO Publishing Company, visit **www.abdopub.com** or contact us at:

4940 Viking Drive, Edina, Minnesota 55435 • 1-800-800-1312 • fax: 1-952-831-1632